Shiva

Chanda and Munda were two demon brothers. They were ferocious and very dangerous. They created havoc in the world. They often interrupted the holy rituals of the sages and killed or wounded innocent people.

All the people prayed to Goddess Shakti to help them. She took pity on them and agreed to help them.

She became very angry on witnessing the havoc the demon brothers had created. Goddess Shakti soon took the form of Goddess Chamunda.

She fought a vicious and horrifying war with Chanda and Munda. The demon brothers, ultimately, lost to the Goddess.

After slaying the demons, the Goddess looked around herself. She was shocked to see that the people living on earth were plagued by greed, jealousy and anger.

The Goddess could not control her temper. She wanted to destroy everything! Lord Shiva sensed her anger and wanted to calm her down.

Suddenly, Lord Shiva got an idea. He went near the forest where the Goddess was present. He, then, transformed himself into a small child.

As soon as he saw the Goddess approaching, he started crying very loudly!

The Goddess was walking when she heard a child cry. She looked around, and spotted the child under a tree.

The Goddess picked up the child
in her arms to calm him down.

The child on seeing her grinned! The Goddess realised that she was the mother to all the human beings on earth.

The Goddess realised her mistake and calmed down. Peace was restored on earth again. Shiva changed into his original form and returned to Kailash Mountain, his home in the Himalayas.